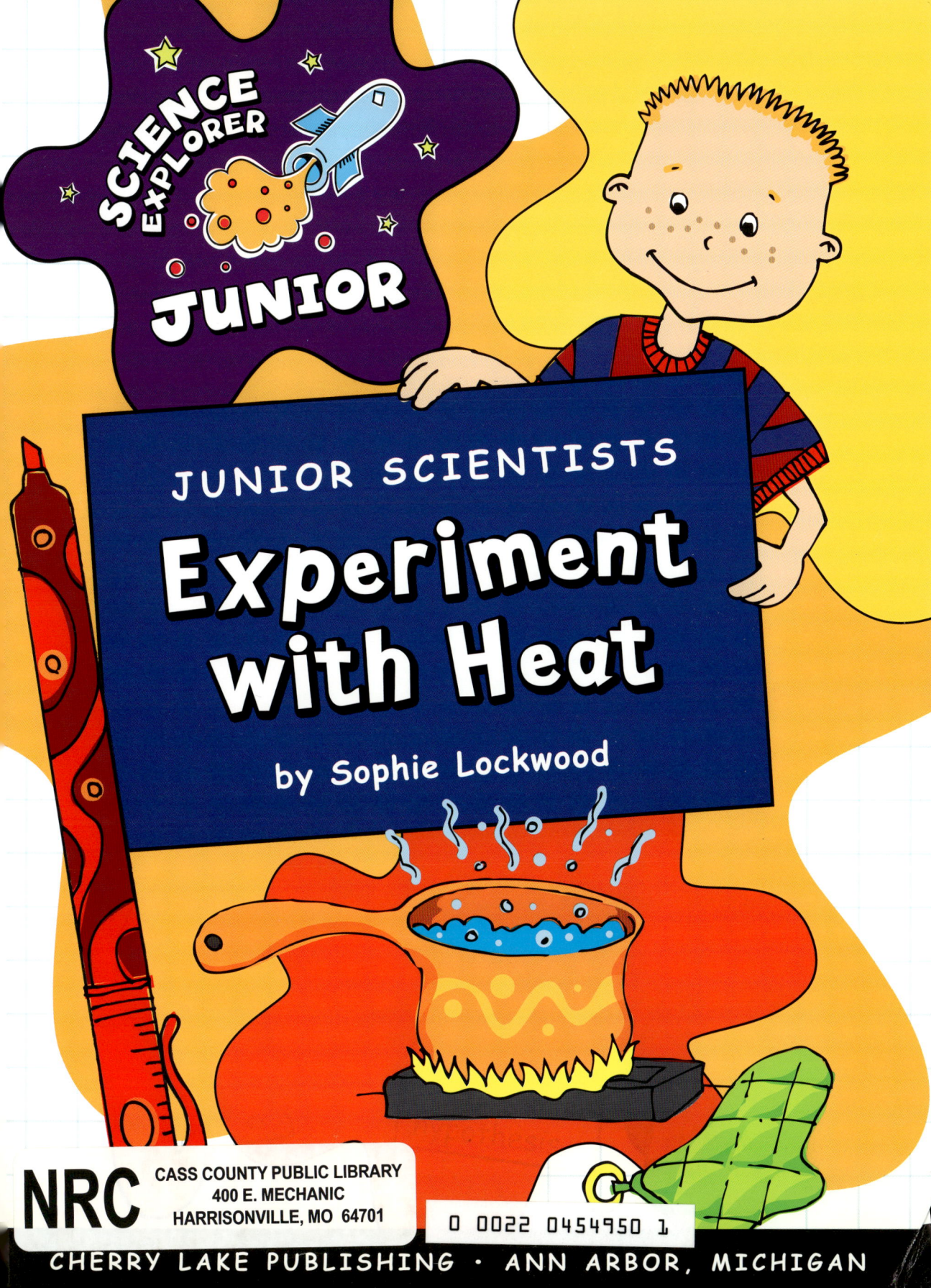

NOTE TO PARENTS AND TEACHERS: Please review the instructions for these experiments before your children do them. Be sure to help them with any experiments you do not think they can safely conduct on their own.

NOTE TO KIDS: Be sure to ask an adult for help with these experiments. Always put your safety first!

Published in the United States of America by Cherry Lake Publishing
Ann Arbor, Michigan
www.cherrylakepublishing.com

Content Editor: Robert Wolffe, EdD, Professor of Teacher Education, Bradley University, Peoria, Illinois
Reading Adviser: Cecilia Minden-Cupp, PhD, Literacy Consultant

Design and Illustration: The Design Lab

Photo Credits: Page 10, ©iStockphoto.com/orangelinemedia; page 15, ©iStockphoto.com/Ulga; page 16, ©iStockphoto.com/Mari; page 23, ©iStockphoto.com/sandsun; page 29, ©Morgan Lane Photography/Shutterstock, Inc.

Copyright ©2011 by Cherry Lake Publishing
All rights reserved. No part of this book may be reproduced or utilized in any form or by any means without written permission from the publisher.

Library of Congress Cataloging-in-Publication Data
Lockwood, Sophie.
  Junior scientists. Experiment with heat / by Sophie Lockwood.
     p. cm.—(Science explorer junior)
  Includes bibliographical references and index.
  ISBN-13: 978-1-60279-843-4 (lib. bdg.)
  ISBN-10: 1-60279-843-5 (lib. bdg.)
  1. Heat—Experiments—Juvenile literature. 2. Science projects—Juvenile literature. I. Title. II. Title: Experiment with heat. III. Series.
  QC256.L62 2010
  536.078—dc22   2009048832

Portions of the text have previously appeared in *Super Cool Science Experiments: Heat* published by Cherry Lake Publishing.

Cherry Lake Publishing would like to acknowledge the work of The Partnership for 21st Century Skills. Please visit www.21stcenturyskills.org for more information.

Printed in the United States of America
Corporate Graphics Inc.
July 2010
CLFA07

TABLE OF CONTENTS

Let's Experiment! 4

EXPERIMENT #1
The Temperature is Rising 10

EXPERIMENT #2
Keeping It Warm 16

EXPERIMENT #3
Heat It Up! 22

Do It Yourself!. 29

Glossary 30
For More Information 31
Index 32
About the Author 32

Let's Experiment!

Doing experiments is fun!

Have you ever done a science **experiment**? They can be lots of fun! You can use experiments to learn about almost anything.

Good scientists observe the world around them.

This book will help you learn how to think like a scientist. Scientists have a special way of learning new things. Some people call it the Scientific Method. This is how it often works:

- Scientists notice things. They **observe** the world around them. They ask questions about things they see, hear, taste, touch, or smell. They come up with problems they would like to solve.

LET'S EXPERIMENT!

- They gather information. They use what they already know to guess the answers to their questions. This kind of guess is called a **hypothesis**.
- Then they test their ideas. They perform experiments or build models. They watch and write down what happens. They learn from each new test.

- They think about what they learned and reach a **conclusion**. This means they come up with an answer to their question. Sometimes they **conclude** that they need to do more experiments!

LET'S EXPERIMENT!

We will use the scientific method to learn more about heat. Heat affects almost everything in our world. We feel it in the weather. We use it to prepare food. Our bodies make heat. Have you ever wondered just how heat works? Why do some things get hot faster than others?

How do you feel when it is really hot outside?

Why do some things protect us from heat? Why do some things keep us warm when it is cold outside? We can answer these questions by doing experiments. Each experiment will teach us something new about heat. Are you ready to be a scientist?

EXPERIMENT #1

The Temperature Is Rising

You use heat to cook food.

First, what do you know about heat? Have you ever watched your parents make dinner? Did you notice that they use heat to cook the food? They do this by putting food into an oven or on a hot stove. They use dishes made of metal, glass, or ceramic. Why do you think this is?

Certain materials are better with heat than others. These things are called **conductors**. As conductors heat up, so does anything that touches them. Metal, glass, and ceramic are good conductors. Do you think plastic is a good conductor? What about wood? Do you think either of them is better than metal?

Let's do an experiment to find out. First, we have to choose a hypothesis:
1. Metal will conduct heat better than plastic or wood.
2. Plastic will conduct heat better than metal or wood.
3. Wood will conduct heat better than metal or plastic.

Let's find out which one is correct!

Which hypothesis do you think is correct?

EXPERIMENT #1: THE TEMPERATURE IS RISING

Here's what you'll need:
- An adult helper
- Butter
- 3 small plastic beads
- 3 spoons of the same length (1 metal, 1 plastic, and 1 wood)
- 1 small, heatproof glass bowl
- 1 potholder
- Hot, boiled water

Ask an adult to help you.

Instructions:
1. Put a dab of butter on the end of each spoon's handle.
2. Stick a bead onto each dab of butter.
3. Put the heatproof glass bowl on the potholder.
4. Place the spoons in the bowl. Make sure the handles are sticking out above the rim of the bowl.

Follow the instructions to set up your experiment.

EXPERIMENT #1: THE TEMPERATURE IS RISING

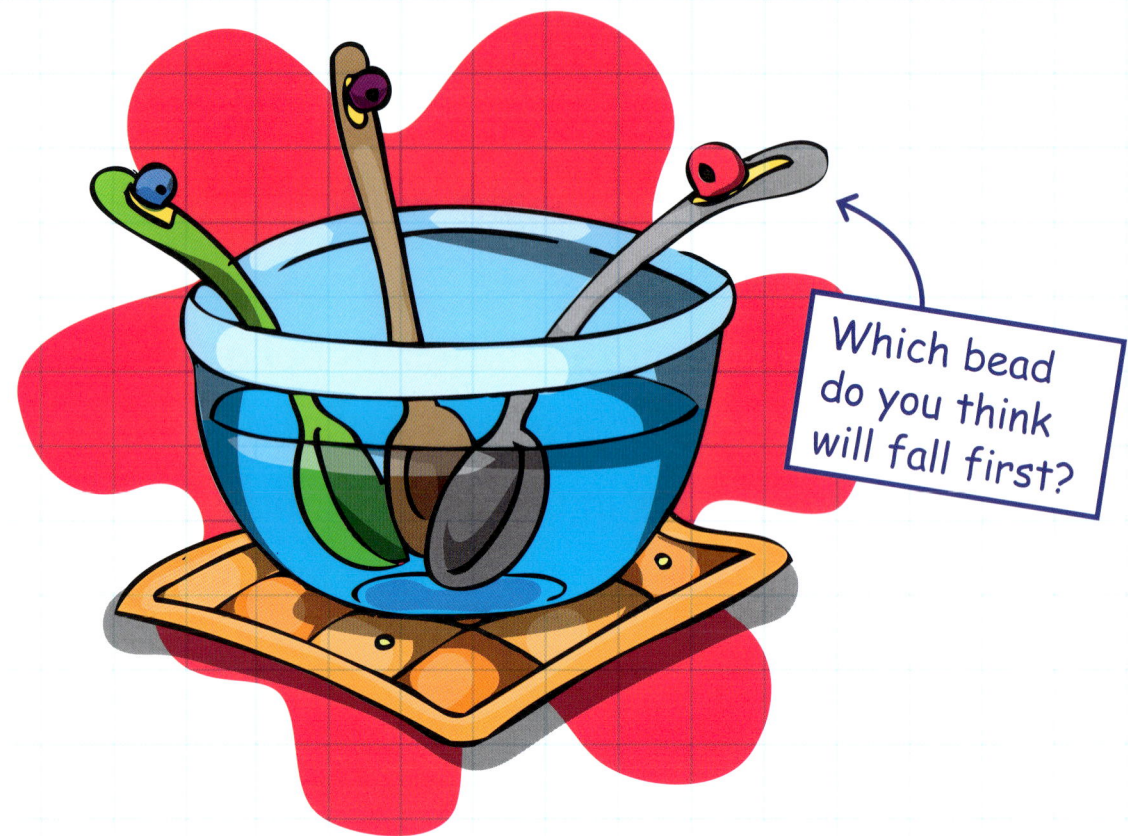

5. Ask an adult to pour a cup of hot water into the bowl. It should be just enough to cover the ends of the spoons. You don't want the handles to be in the water.

6. Watch what happens. The butter will start to melt as each spoon conducts heat from the water. The bead stuck onto the butter will fall when the butter melts. Which bead do you think will fall first?

Conclusion:

Which bead dropped first? Was it the one on the metal spoon? Did you prove your hypothesis? Now you know one reason why people use metal pans to cook!

Metal pans are good heat conductors.

EXPERIMENT #2

Keeping It Warm

Do you wear an insulator when you go outside?

You just learned that you can use a conductor to heat something up. How do you keep something warm? Materials that keep heat in are called **insulators**. Your winter coat insulates you from the cold.

Good insulators do not conduct heat. Instead, they trap air around the hot substance. Let's experiment to find out what materials are good insulators. You will wrap three coffee cups with different materials. Which one will be the best insulator? Think about Experiment #2. Which spoons did not conduct heat well? Does that give you a clue?

Let's choose a hypothesis:
1. Plastic is a better insulator than cotton or metal.
2. Cotton is a better insulator than plastic or metal.
3. Metal is a better insulator than plastic or cotton.

Let's get started!

Record your hypothesis.

EXPERIMENT #2: KEEPING IT WARM

Collect your supplies.

Here's what you'll need:
- 3 coffee mugs of the same size
- Cellophane tape
- Aluminum foil
- A small plastic trash bag
- An old cotton sock
- Very hot water
- Scissors
- Thermometer

Instructions:

1. Cut a piece of aluminum foil. Wrap it around the outside of a coffee mug. Make sure it fits all the way around the mug. Use tape to hold the aluminum foil in place if you need to.
2. Cut a piece out of the plastic bag. Wrap it around a second mug.

Wrap each mug carefully.

EXPERIMENT #2: KEEPING IT WARM

3. Cut the bottom off a sock. Slide the top portion around the third mug. Use tape to hold it in place if you need to.
4. Have an adult help you carefully fill each mug with the same amount of hot water.
5. Wait 15 minutes. Then use the thermometer to measure the temperature of the water in each cup. Write down your results.

Check the temperature of the water in each cup.

Conclusion:

Which mug has the hottest water? The material wrapped around that mug is the best insulator of the three. Was your hypothesis correct? Write down your conclusions.

EXPERIMENT #3

Heat It Up!

Ice cream melts quickly on hot days.

Have you ever tried to eat ice cream on a hot day? Did the ice cream melt when it got too warm? Heat can cause many things to change shape. This is called a physical change. The ice cream isn't solid anymore, but it is still ice cream.

Do you think some things can go back to the way they were? An experiment can help us find out the answer. Start by choosing a hypothesis:

1. Changes that take place when objects are heated cannot be changed back.
2. Changes that take place when objects are heated can sometimes be changed back.

Let's get started!

Do you think melted ice can go back to being an ice cube?

EXPERIMENT #3: HEAT IT UP!

Here's what you'll need:

- Three pieces of aluminum foil, 3 inches by 3 inches (7.6 centimeters by 7.6 cm)
- An unwrapped piece of chocolate
- An unwrapped crayon
- An ice cube
- A desk lamp with a flexible arm
- A timer

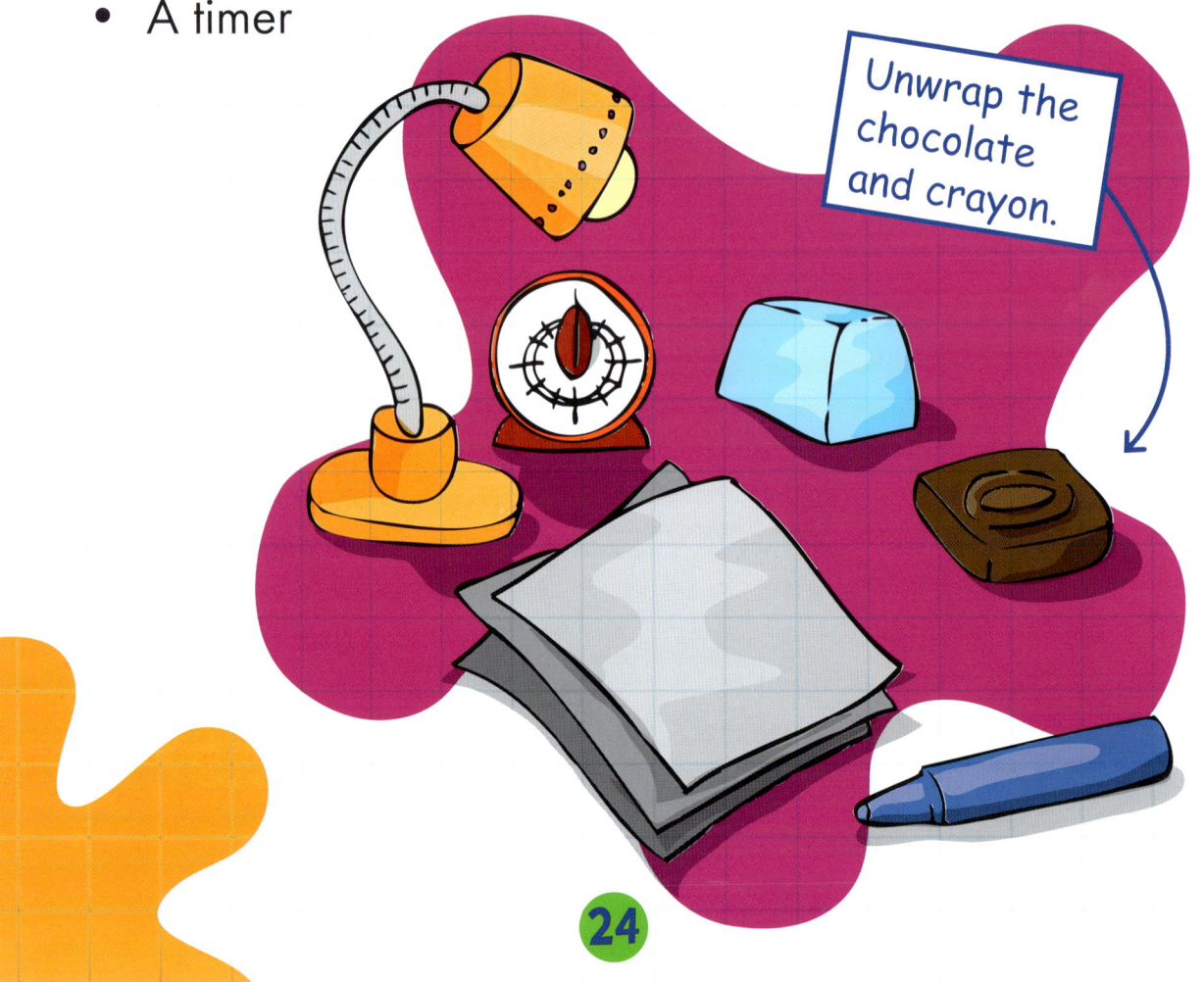

Unwrap the chocolate and crayon.

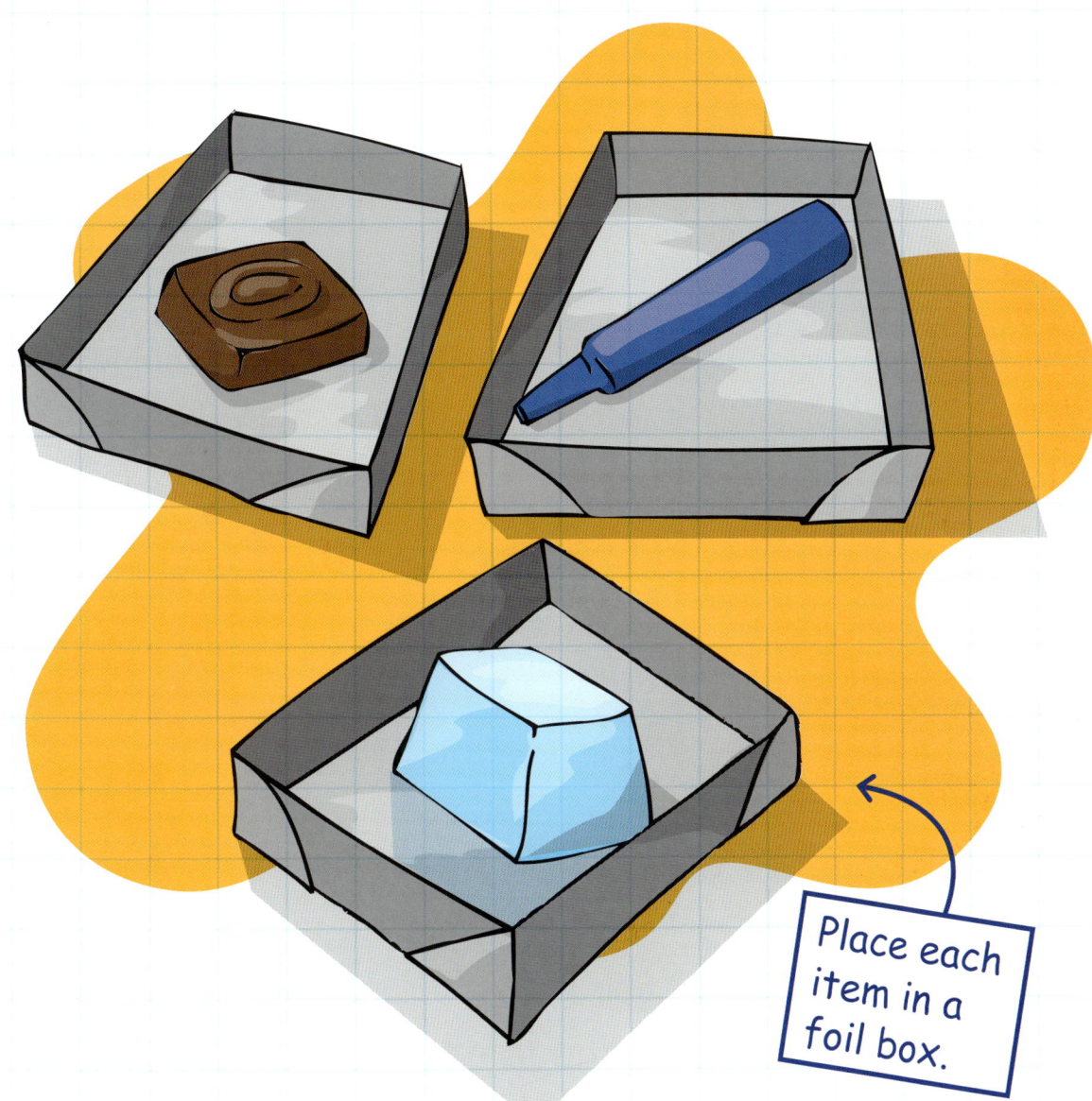

Place each item in a foil box.

Instructions:
1. First, we need to make foil boxes. Fold up the sides of each piece of foil about ½ inch (1 cm). Then pinch the corners.
2. Put the chocolate in box one, the crayon in box two, and the ice cube in box three.

EXPERIMENT #3: HEAT IT UP!

3. Put box one under the lamp. Ask an adult to help you adjust the lamp. The light bulb should be 2 inches (5 cm) above the box. Use the lamp to heat the box for 5 minutes. What happens to the chocolate? Write down the result.
4. Remove the foil box with the chocolate and put it to the side.

5. Repeat this process with each box. Make sure that each box remains under the light bulb for exactly 5 minutes.
6. After 1 hour, take a look at each box again. Record what you see.

Record what you see in 1 hour.

EXPERIMENT #3: HEAT IT UP!

The crayon may be a different shape, but it turned back into a solid.

Conclusion:

What happened to each item when you heated it up? What happened after the items cooled off? The chocolate and the crayon melted. They turned solid again when they cooled. The ice cube melted and turned into water. You probably know that you can turn water back into ice, though!

This means that the physical changes that happen when something is heated can sometimes be undone. Was your hypothesis correct?

Do It Yourself!

Try your own experiments!

Okay, scientists! Now you know some new things about heat. You learned about conductors and insulators. You also learned that changes caused by heat can sometimes be changed back.

Do you have more questions about heat? Maybe you would like to know if heat will melt certain objects. You might be wondering if some kinds of cloth are better for insulating. Try using the scientific method to answer your questions about heat!

GLOSSARY

conclude (kuhn-KLOOD) to make a final decision based on what you know

conclusion (kuhn-KLOO-zhuhn) final decision, thought, or opinion

conductors (kuhn-DUK-terz) things that allow the transfer of heat or electricity

experiment (ecks-PARE-uh-ment) a scientific way to test a guess about something

hypothesis (hy-POTH-uh-sihss) a guess about what will happen in an experiment

insulators (IN-suh-lay-terz) things that hold heat in

method (METH-uhd) a way of doing something

observe (ob-ZURV) to see something or notice things by using the other senses

predict (pruh-DIKT) to make a guess about what will happen

FOR MORE INFORMATION

BOOKS
Cook, Trevor. *Experiments with Heat*. New York: PowerKids Press, 2009.

Gardner, Robert. *Temperature and Heat: Great Experiments and Ideas*. Berkeley Heights, NJ: Enslow Publishers, 2009.

WEB SITES
All Science Fair Projects—Heat
www.all-science-fair-projects.com/category58.html
Find projects about heat for students of all ages.

Exploratorium Science Snacks—Heat
www.exploratorium.edu/snacks/iconheat.html
Discover 10 easy-to-do experiments involving heat.

INDEX

conclusions, 7, 15, 21, 28

conductors, 11, 14, 17, 29

experiments, 4, 6, 7, 9, 29

hypotheses, 6, 11, 17, 23

insulators, 16–17, 21, 29

models, 6

notes, 6, 20, 21, 26

observations, 5, 14, 29

physical changes, 22–23, 28

questions, 5, 6, 7, 8–9, 11, 17, 23, 29

Scientific Method, 5–8, 29

scientists, 5

supplies, 12, 18, 24

ABOUT THE AUTHOR

Sophie Lockwood has written many books for young readers. She lives in South Carolina with her husband and enjoys reading, playing bridge, and watching movies when she isn't writing.